FOR GOD & TSAR

A Brief History of Russian America, 1741-1867

by
David J. Nordlander

Historian
Sitka National Historical Park
Alaska

The Alaska Natural History Association is a non-profit organization dedicated to enhancing the public's understanding and conservation of Alaska's natural, cultural and historical resources by working in cooperation with land management agencies and other educational organizations throughout Alaska.

Design: David Freeman · Cover Illustration: Dee Boyles · Photos courtesy National Park Service

Published by the Alaska Natural History Association
401 West 1st Avenue, Anchorage, Alaska 99501

Second Printing 1998

ISBN# 0-930931-15-7 Printed in the U.S.A.

CONTENTS

Russian Tsar Peter the Great

The concept of manifest destiny is entwined in the history of Russian America. From the late sixteenth century onward, Russian migration to the east inevitably led to the North Pacific Ocean and Alaska. Indeed, the "discovery" of Alaska came as the end result of an expansionist phenomenon that in itself was a major historical event.[1] In the early fifteenth century, "Russia" consisted of an unconsolidated group of principalities that were just emerging from over two centuries of Mongol conquest, whereby the heirs of Ghengis Khan had previously devastated these regions. While a number of cities such as Novgorod and Kiev held preeminence by their age, it was the relatively young principality of Muscovy (Moscow) that served as the focal point in the defeat of the Mongolian Golden Horde. In the two hundred years following Dmitrii Donskoi's victory over the Mongols at the Battle of Kulikovo in 1380, the Muscovite princes began a process of the "gathering of the Russian lands" that led by the time of Ivan the Terrible (Ivan IV) in the mid-sixteenth century to a strong and centralized political state capable of significant territorial expansion. The first Muscovite grand prince to call himself tsar, Ivan IV pushed Russia eastward by defeating the khanates of Kazan and Astrakhan, remnants of the Mongol Empire, in the 1550s. With the help of the cossack *hetman* Ermak Timofeevich, Ivan subsequently conquered the khanate of Sibir´ (Siberia) to the east of the Ural Mountains by 1581. In the succeeding century, the Russians continued explorations from there and reached the Pacific Ocean in 1639.

The impetus for this movement east came from a number of sources. Certainly, the thirst for riches, particularly in the form of the luxurious pelt of the sable, drove numerous cossacks and other frontiersmen to explore the edge of the Russian Empire. At the same time, however, tsarist policy from the era of Ivan the Terrible to that of Peter the Great (Peter I) also prodded Russians onward to discover new and distant realms.[2] Pushed by the twin goals of territorial conquest

1

and geographical interest, the tsars both commanded and financed exploratory missions to the terra incognita that was the eastern border of Russia.[3] Expanding upon Ivan's initiative, Peter continued tsarist expansionism beyond the shores of the North Pacific. Famous for his obsession with Western Europe, Peter was also fascinated by the unknown land that lay on the eastern edge of his dominions. In 1725, as his last official act, he commissioned an expedition that was to investigate the territory beyond the Russian Far East.[4]

✦ II. BERING'S VOYAGES TO ALASKA ✦

Following Peter's death in 1725, the First Kamchatka Expedition, named for the eastern Russian peninsula that was the base of explorations, set out with the Danish captain Vitus Bering as its commander. Serving in the Imperial Russian Navy, Bering had distinguished himself in Peter's Northern War against Sweden as a capable and reliable officer. Peter's selection of Bering as leader of the Pacific mission derived from this earlier success. In any event, after an extensive and difficult overland journey through Siberia from the Russian capital of St. Petersburg, Bering sailed into the narrow straits that separate the continents of Asia and America. In 1728, he tentatively concluded that these great landmasses were not connected, though he knew not what lay beyond.[5]

Upon Bering's return to European Russia, however, the Imperial Academy of Sciences deemed his findings unsatisfactory. The Academy decided that further research and exploration were necessary to conclusively determine the answer to Peter's original questions. Since 1648, nebulous rumors had circulated in Russia about this region from an earlier expedition in the North Pacific under the com-

European map from 1714, "The Great Unknown" of Northwestern America

mand of Simeon Dezhnev. The tsarist government wanted confirmatory evidence, and thus sent Bering on a Second Kamchatka Expedition in the 1730's.

After traveling many years through virtually untrodden Siberian territory with men and equipment, this expedition finally departed from Petropavlovsk on the Kamchatka Peninsula in June 1741. Comprised of two packet boats, the *St. Peter* under Bering's command, and the *St. Paul* under his assistant Aleksei Chirikov, this second exploration was successful in its mission in spite of the fact that the two boats were separated by tempestuous weather soon after their departure from Kamchatka. On July 15, Chirikov sighted land in the vicinity of present-day souteast Alaska, while Bering viewed the impressive coastal mountains of northern southeast Alaska the following day, naming the highest peak Mount St. Elias in honor of that saint's nameday on the Russian Orthodox calendar.[6]

Though Bering died on the return voyage to Kamchatka in December 1741, his crew and that of Chirikov returned to Russia with tales of the mysterious northeast. Perhaps more important than the scientific findings that drove the exploration, however, were the 600 rich pelts of the sea otter that the Russians brought home. Luxurious and rare, these furs caused a sensation in European Russia. For years, Russian traders and trappers had sought the pelt of the sable across northern Russia and Siberia. Indeed, sable had been a basic item in trade with the nations of Europe, particularly in the Hanseatic League's outpost at Novgorod. At this time, merchants evaluated the fur of the sea otter as possessing even higher value than that of the sable, particularly in the markets of China and the Far East. In light of this and the fact that the Russians had hunted the sable to near extinction, the discovery of valuable sea otters off the coast of Alaska met with interest and jubilation in Russia.

✦ III. THE FIRST KLONDIKE ✦

Without question, the prospect of unlimited commercial wealth drove many Russians to Alaska over the course of the next century.[7] Between the early 1740s and the late 1770s, Russian merchants and trappers came in successive waves along the Aleutian Islands in search of personal fortunes, much as those who went to the Klondike (Yukon Territory) in 1898 to find gold. Sailing on unreliable *shitki* (small boats made of logs lashed together by rope), new Russian settlers harvested the natural bounty of the Aleutian chain island by island until they reached the vicinity of Kodiak in the 1770s. But government expeditions also continued, including one by P.K. Krenitsyn in 1768-69 and another by I.I. Billings and G.A. Sarychev in the 1780s.

The question thus arises: What factor served the key role in the subsequent Russian colonization of Alaska? Undeniably, the Russian tsars played a major part in encouraging and supporting the drive to and across the Pacific. After all, official government exploratory voyages made possible the Russian settling of Alaska. In essence, however, Russian expansionism to the east was dictated more by the personal interest and need of individual Russians who ventured into the New World than by state initiative.

Besides the prospect of commercial wealth, many Russians had other reasons for undertaking the long eastward trek. Of these, the greatest may have been the

chance for social advancement. In the eighteenth century, Russia was a highly
rigid and stratified society. In the eyes of the government, particularly under the
Empress Catherine the Great (Catherine II), the population was divided into three
estates: the nobility, townsmen, and state peasantry. (Serfs, the majority of the
Russian people, did not even rate a classification.) Each estate had rights and
privileges pursuant to social position. For men of low birth, Siberia and Alaska
offered upward mobility and a change in fortune and status. In many ways, this
phenomenon was similar to the one that drew pioneers to the American West in
the nineteenth century. In any event, from the cossacks of the sixteenth century to
the merchants of the eighteenth and nineteenth centuries, the eastern frontier of
Russia offered opportunities for advancement that were unavailable to those who
remained in the socially stratified provinces of European Russia.

Beyond these motives, however, commercial wealth stood as the most vital
impetus toward the Russian colonization of Alaska. In the first few decades after
Bering's voyage, a number of self-sufficient frontiersmen known as *promyshlenniki*
came to the Aleutians in search of the valuable sea otter. Of course, the risks of
their journey matched the potential rewards that awaited them. Because the trip
across the North Pacific in their makeshift boats was highly dangerous, many lost
their lives before reaching the distant shores. But since the *promyshlenniki* had
always led the pursuit of the sable across northern Russia and Siberia, it was only
natural that these men would be the first Russians to capitalize upon the
resources of Alaska. The prospect of great wealth ensured that a continual supply
of colonists would repeat the treacherous crossing. But greed and frontier cruelty
unfortunately caused many of the earliest arrivals to exploit both the native populations and the wilderness without sufficient regard for their wellbeing. Both
Aleut and sea otter populations quickly plummeted.[8]

Sea Otter, the "Soft Gold"

Aleut hunter in traditional garb

✦ IV. RUSSIAN CAPITALISM IN ALASKA ✦

While these initial "entrepreneurs" were economically successful in their own way, it was apparent by the 1760s and 1770s that ever larger ventures would be needed to organize and finance Russian commercial activity in Alaska.[9] Consequently, corporate associations began to take the place of independent initiative on the Aleutian Islands. Joint-stock companies, with their main offices and boards of directors typically in St. Petersburg and branch offices in the eastern Siberian city of Irkutsk, became the dominant form of Russian commercialism throughout Alaska. Though Soviet historians continually debated the question of the origin of capitalism in the heartland of Russia, there is no doubt that capitalism played the major role in the earliest years of the history of Russian America.

Aside from the economic aspects of this activity, the dominance of Russian joint-stock companies in Alaska held a larger import as well. In 1762, Catherine the Great came to power in Russia after the premature death (at the hands of Catherine's supporters) of her husband, Tsar Peter III. Fancying herself an intellectual, particularly after lengthy correspondence with the great French philosophés such as Voltaire and Diderot, the ambitious Catherine came to accept in principle many of the economic ideas then current in Western Europe. Though some companies tried to gain particular favor with the tsarist government, Catherine announced that there would be free competition, and thus no state-sponsored subsidies or monopolies, throughout the Russian Empire. Most importantly, the Russian state would play a minor role in the far-eastern realms of the country. As a result, private corporations not only had the chance to turn a profit, but also became the *de facto* governments in their various spheres of activity in the American colony.

In actuality, this also meant that private capital served as the backbone of Russian economic activity in the New World. While the tsar or tsarina may have later offered privileges and protection, the funding of ventures in Russian America came from the investments of shareholders in the companies that operated in Alaska. Along with this funding came control, for the simple reason that no rival authority existed in the colony. Some historians have nevertheless contended that the tsarist government exercised direct supervision over the Alaskan operations, albeit surreptitiously.[10] Available evidence suggests, however, that the various corporations fulfilled the primary role in the territory, with the tsar functioning in a largely supportive context.[11] In any case, privately-raised capital,

Russian boat-building facility at Resurrection Bay on the Kenai Peninsula

Grigorii Shelikhov, founder of the Russian American Company

supported official enterprises throughout the history of Russian America, including the extensive work in later years of the Russian Orthodox Church. Corporate directors consequently exerted a tremendous amount of influence in their respective venues of operation.

By the 1780s, there were six Russian joint-stock companies active in Alaska, all named after the men who founded them: Shelikhov-Golikov, Lebedev-Lastochkin, Panov, Orechov, Kiselev, and Alin. Carving out their own niches, each corporation occupied different regions of Alaska from the Aleutian Islands to Prince William Sound. Of these, the largest were the Lebedev-Lastochkin Company, centered on the Kenai Peninsula, and the Shelikhov-Golikov Company, headquartered on Kodiak Island. Quite naturally, they became fierce and uncompromising rivals.

In the late 1780s, the Irkutsk merchant who was the mastermind behind the latter company, Grigorii Shelikhov, traveled to St. Petersburg in an attempt to win tsarist favor in his competition with the other Russian companies in Alaska. Upon arrival in the Russian imperial capital, he petitioned Catherine to grant a state-sponsored monopoly to his company. She refused his request because of her economic beliefs. Disappointed and weary, Shelikhov returned to Alaska empty-handed. Events in the near future, however, would help reverse his fortune.[12]

✦ V. BIRTH OF THE RUSSIAN AMERICAN COMPANY ✦

The critical moment came when Catherine the Great died in 1796. Succeeding her to the Russian throne, her son Paul I made a sudden and radical break with the policies of his mother. Most historians attribute this to Paul's intense hatred of Catherine and her intrigues (she may have killed his father, Peter

III, and prevented Paul from becoming tsar for over twenty years). In any event, his reversals of official state doctrine held great ramifications for the course of events in Alaska. By 1799, Paul agreed to issue a charter granting a monopoly of economic activity in Russian America to the Shelikhov-Golikov Company. Henceforth, this corporation would be known as the Russian American Company, with exclusive privileges to exploit the resources of Russia's overseas colony. The new tsar gave all other Russian companies active in Alaska a choice: merge their operations with those of Shelikhov-Golikov, or liquidate their assets.[13]

In many respects, the issuance of a tsarist charter of monopoly in 1799 was the result of a twist of political fate in the Russian capital of St. Petersburg. On the other hand, however, it was an admission of economic reality. Over the years, ever greater amounts of Russian capital were needed in Alaska to exploit the natural resources. This was the reason that organized corporations had succeeded the solitary activities of the *promyshlenniki* by the 1770s. Toward the turn of the nineteenth century, however, even these corporate ventures were struggling to turn a profit, with only the Shelikhov-Golikov and Lebedev-Lastochkin Companies in somewhat stable economic positions. Eventually, the tsarist government recognized that if operations in Alaska were to continue to be profitable in the future, the Russian state would have to choose a single company that it would supply with privileges and protection.[14]

The reason that the tsar chose the Shelikhov-Golikov Company to be the recipient of a state-sponsored monopoly, though, likely had as much to do with Grigorii Shelikhov's ingratiating persistence in the imperial court of the Russian capital as anything else.[15] Nevertheless, there were sufficient economic justifications for this

Kodiak, the first colonial capital of Russian America

decision as well. From nearly the beginning of its existence, the Shelikhov-Golikov Company had been relatively robust. Over the years, Shelikhov proved himself to be a talented businessman, albeit a cruel and often unscrupulous one. Basing his operations at Three Saints Bay on Kodiak Island, he reaped many profits throughout the 1780s and 1790s. This location was auspicious, giving him proximity to both the Pacific Ocean, with its abundance of valuable sea otter, and the Alaskan mainland, where foxes and other fur-bearing animals could be successfully pursued.

Shelikhov's community on Kodiak was also thriving in other ways that attracted the attention of the Russian tsars: namely, he built a school for Alaskan native children, and purported that a thriving Russian Orthodox community on Kodiak had been established through his own personal missionary activity. Most historians think this was done to satisfy the idealistic goals of Catherine the Great, who had admonished the Russians to treat the natives of Alaska with both humanity and Christian humility.[16]

In spite of suspect motives, Shelikhov was nevertheless successful in his intentions. Though he died in 1795, the tsarist government deemed his company the most worthy of a monopoly in 1799. Thereafter, the renamed Russian American Company continued to be a successful venture for another half-century. Relieved of its rivals, it turned profits that delighted its board of directors and shareholders back in St. Petersburg. Furthermore, it served as a valuable political outpost on the eastern frontier of the Russian Empire by extending Russia's influence in the New World and limiting the prospects of its major European competitors, particularly Great Britain. Some Russians even viewed Alaska as the foundation of a prosperous and growing Russian colony that would successfully compete with the other colonies of North America.

✦ VI. DREAMS OF A RUSSIAN EMPIRE IN NORTH AMERICA ✦

The main proponent of this view was Nikolai Rezanov, *Ober-Prokuror* (Chief Procurator) of the Imperial Russian Senate and a close confidant of the Russian tsar, Aleksandr I, in the early nineteenth century. Rezanov proposed that the Russian government extend its Alaskan colony as far south as Northern California in order to increase both its economic and political prospects among the rival European powers on the North American continent. To this end, Rezanov traveled to the *presidio* at San Francisco in 1806 to negotiate with the Spanish authorities on the possibilities of such a venture. Furthermore, he envisioned a Russian toehold in Hawaii that would solidify for Russia a major role in the Pacific. Though his results were indeterminate, Rezanov left California with the notion of a potentially mighty Russian presence in the New World intact.[17]

Though Rezanov's vision of a glorious North American empire was not unique among Russian statesmen, his activity towards its realization was by far the most significant. Nevertheless, other Russian authorities preceded him in advocating the expansion of Russian influence and culture in the New World. Of these, the foremost was the Russian Orthodox Church. In 1794, Russian Orthodoxy officially came to Alaska with the arrival at Kodiak of ten missionaries from the Valaam monastery near St. Petersburg.[18] Although Shelikhov's claims to Catherine the Great of a mature religious colony with actual churches on Kodiak Island proved to be bogus, the new missionaries quickly set to work on an expansive evangelical effort that would bring not only Orthodoxy to the vast territory of Alaska, but Russian culture as well. By the middle of the nineteenth century, the Russian church was active in all areas of Russian inhabitation or exploration in Alaska, from the Yup'ik Eskimo villages of the Yukon Delta to the Pribilov and Aleutian Islands, and from the Kenai Peninsula to Kodiak and southeastern Alaska. Of all the Russian institutions in Alaskan history, the Russian Orthodox Church proved to be the most long-lasting, retaining a significant influence among native Alaskans even to the present day.[19]

✦ VII. RUSSIAN OUTPOSTS IN CALIFORNIA AND HAWAII ✦

While Orthodoxy prospered, however, Rezanov's dreams did not. During his return to St. Petersburg from North America, he died on the long overland journey through Siberia. Russia's American colony was never to see a higher-placed advocate than Rezanov, and his death certainly dimmed the prospects for the expansion of the Russian Empire into other parts of the New World. Rezanov's vision of a contiguous Russian territory from Alaska to Northern California was never realized. Nevertheless, some of his hopes were fulfilled; in 1812, Ivan Kuskov built a Russian settlement at Fort Ross (*krepost' rus'*) on the California coast, about eighty miles north of San Francisco. Establishment of a base in California offered the Russians continuous proximity to valuable new hunting grounds for the sea otter, which were soon plied by their Aleut and Kenaitze hunters. Beyond this was a more pressing hope that this southern outpost could supply the Alaskan colony with adequate foodstuffs. As a result, wheat fields were planted outside the palisades and ranches farmed in the immediate vicinity.

Russian settlement at Fort Ross, California

The protracted need for provisions in Russian America stemmed from a number of reasons, with the primary one being the Russian inability to adapt to native diets. Obviously the Tlingit and other indigenous peoples of Alaska had survived quite adequately for thousands of years by utilizing the natural foods of their environment. As newcomers, the Russians brought their own traditional dietary needs that centered around grains, fruits, vegetables, and beef not native to this region of the New World. Over the course of time, only one of their familiar staples, potatoes, grew with any success in the northern climate. Eager to raise grain and other crops suitable to their tastes, the Russians looked to temperate California for a solution. They envisioned Fort Ross as the breadbasket for Alaska.[20]

The colonial administration felt desperate. Earlier ideas had proven unsuccessful. From 1795-1806, the Russians had developed an agricultural settlement named *Slavarossii* (Glory of Russia) at Yakutat, Alaska with a contingent of serfs whom Catherine the Great allowed Shelikhov to purchase.[21] Marginally useful, this village was destroyed by the native Tlingit in 1806.[22] Soon thereafter, the development of a Russian village in California seemed a logical solution. But Fort Ross never fulfilled its expected potential in supplying Russian America with adequate foodstuffs. While initially successful, Fort Ross continually ran into red ink by the 1830s and was sold to an American entrepreneur, John Sutter, in 1841. From that point on, the Russian American Company met its need for staples through trade with the Hudson's Bay Company and with the Sandwich Islands (Hawaii).

Rezanov's hopes for a Russian base in Hawaii were also temporarily realized in 1815 with the establishment of a stone fort on the island of Kauai. This venture, however, proved to be exceedingly short-lived; having raised the ire of King Kamehameha on the neighboring island of Oahu, the settlement was terminated in 1817.[23] Other than Fort Ross, the Russian presence in the New World would thereafter be restricted to Alaska. In many ways, though, this was not a setback for the Russian American Company. As with most Russian corporate ventures that came to Alaska, the company was primarily interested in turning a commercial profit. The political goals of Rezanov, while providing some economic benefit in access to the waters off the California coast, went beyond the main interests of the corporate leadership. After all, the resources of Alaska had hardly been tapped to their full extent. Consequently, the company refocused its efforts in the early years of the nineteenth century on the coastal area of southeastern Alaska.

✦ VIII. A NEW CAPITAL FOR RUSSIAN AMERICA ✦

By the end of the eighteenth century, the waters off Kodiak Island had been significantly depleted of the valuable sea otter that originally brought the Russians to Alaska in ever greater numbers over the preceding fifty years. Aleksandr Baranov, whom Shelikhov had named the Chief Manager (*Glavnyi pravitel'*) of his company in 1790, determined that the center of Russian operations would need to move to southeastern Alaska in the near future if the Russian American Company were to continue turning a profit. Latching upon Rezanov's aims of expanding Russia's political sovereignty in the New World, Baranov advocated establishing a settlement in the vicinity of present-day Sitka. In 1799, he

Aleksandr Baranov, first Chief Manager of the Russian American Company

built a fortified redoubt (Old Sitka) seven miles north of a native Tlingit village, "Shee-Atika." While the Tlingit destroyed this fort and massacred most of its inhabitants in 1802, Baranov resolved to return. In spite of justifiable native claims against the Russian invasion of their territory, Baranov used the massacre as a pretext and attacked the Tlingit stronghold in 1804 with the help of the gunship *Neva* (which had recently been the first Russian vessel to circumnavigate the globe). Russian cannons eventually prevailed, and the Tlingit under Katlian, their chief, had to withdraw into the forests. At the conclusion of the Battle of Sitka, the company reestablished a Russian town on the site of the Tlingit village. Naming it *Novo-Arkhangel'sk* (New Archangel), the administration made this city the capital of Russian America in 1808.[24]

The transfer of the Russian colonial capital from Kodiak to New Archangel was primarily carried out for economic reasons. While Rezanov had advocated moving the capital for political advantage in expanding the southern territory of Russia's American possessions, Baranov and the corporate leadership of the Russian American Company saw in New Archangel the potential advancement of several economic interests: (1) New Archangel's coastal waters possessed an untapped source of the sea otter, now nearly depleted off the Aleutians and Kodiak; (2) the new Russian settlement had an excellent natural harbor; (3) New Archangel also possessed a prime location for trade as it was on a major European water route in the Pacific; (4) finally, the city was in a strategic position to guard the southern boundaries of Russia's colony, claimed by the European right of discovery, from intruding British and American traders. For those with vested financial interests, the long-term economic health of the Russian American Company appeared to hang on the relocation of the capital to New Archangel.

✦ IX. RUSSIAN ALASKAN GOVERNORS ✦

Over the course of the next several decades, New Archangel developed into the most sophisticated of the Russian settlements in the New World. Whereas Kodiak retained a simpler social character due to the presence of many lower-class Russians who originally came to Alaska in search of wealth and a change in personal fortune, New Archangel became the symbol of a new glittering colonial aristocracy emerging in the Alaskan wilderness. Gradually, elites of the Russian nobility replaced the *promyshlenniki* of an earlier and humbler era. Military officers, particularly of the Imperial Russian Navy, began to serve in the highest echelons of the Russian American Company. In fact, the successors to Baranov as Chief Managers (governors) of the company were naval officers, often with the status of nobility. Although serving as Chief Manager for twenty-seven years, Baranov himself was a symbol of the old days in the eyes of his successors.

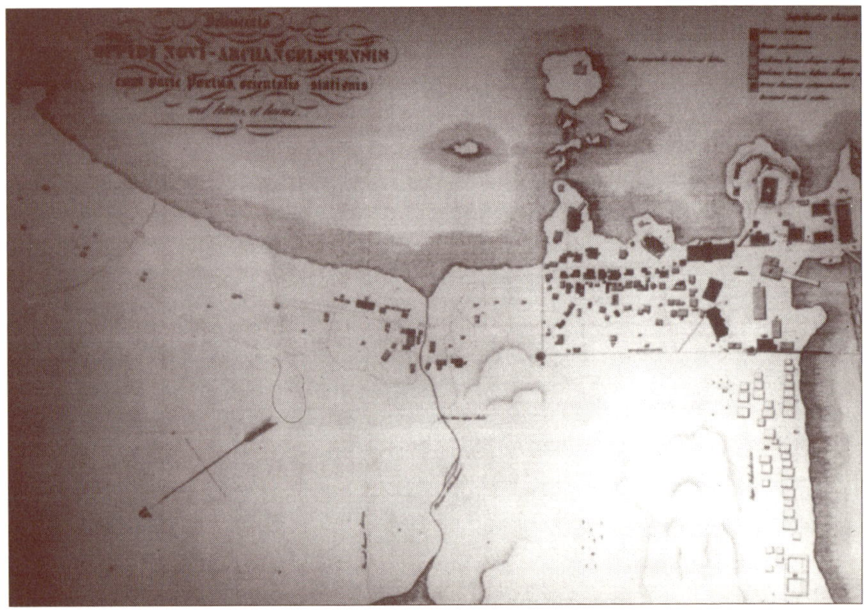

Map of New Archangel, second Russian colonial capital, in the 1840s

13

"Baranov's Castle" in New Archangel

The Russian officers consistently looked down on him as a man of inferior position; after all, he was of the hereditary rank of *meshchannin,* or the non-privileged merchantry.[25]

In 1818, Baranov retired and set out for European Russia after nearly thirty years of service in Alaska. He died at sea, however, while on a company vessel in the vicinity of Java in the Indian Ocean. Despite Baranov's long years of leadership, the company authorities in St. Petersburg quickly forgot about him. While Baranov left a mixed legacy that included some unfortunate mistreatment of the native populations, he had been highly successful as the Chief Manager of the Russian American Company. Indeed, his business acumen and scrupulous financial honesty had caused the board of directors to plead with him to stay on in Alaska even though Baranov had sought retirement as early as 1810. But the company was not overly sentimental, and his services were seen as ultimately replaceable. Even his death at sea brought only a perfunctory response from the corporate headquarters in the form of a brief obituary. The directors most likely held the notion that the naval officers would certainly exceed the lowly Baranov in the management of their business affairs.

The course of time proved them wrong. Indeed, few of Baranov's successors matched his abilities at running the Russian American Company. His immediate replacement, a Baltic German named Leontii Hagemeister, was a managerial failure. The men who followed him throughout the 1820s were not much better. What the naval officers did manage to do was import an aristocratic society to the fringes of the Russian Empire. Accustomed to the imperial court of St. Petersburg,

Arvid Etholen, a Finn who was Chief Manager of the Russian American Company in the 1840s

the new leaders simply recreated their social privileges in the microcosm of Alaska. By the 1830s, the Chief Managers had replaced Baranov's rudimentary dwelling on a central hill in New Archangel with an impressive, two-story palace that ironically became known as "Baranov's Castle." While most of New Archangel's residents lived in quite humble shelters, the aristocratic naval officers shared a much higher lifestyle that included formal balls and gala receptions. It was for this slice of Russian society that New Archangel became known among visiting sailors and merchants as the "Paris of the Pacific."

Of course, not all of Baranov's successors were business failures; indeed, at least two were quite prominent in their leadership abilities. Baron Ferdinand von Wrangell (1830-1835) and Arvid Adolf Etholen (1840-1845) presided over successful five-year tenures that witnessed a significant expansion in the activities of the Russian American Company. Von Wrangell, a Baltic German, and Etholen, a Finn, were representative of the multi-ethnic character of the Russian military in the early nineteenth century. Encompassing the Grand Duchy of Finland, the Baltic lands, and remnants of Poland, among other territories, the Russian Empire at this time embraced a variety of peoples who, in open competition, often gave the military highly-qualified leadership. Occasionally this translated into effective business talent as well; Etholen was perhaps the most capable Chief Manager of the company after Baranov. In fact, many historians claim that the early 1840s marked the peak of a "golden age" in the Russian presence in Alaska. The company was not only turning a consistent and robust profit, but also was engaged in a large construction boom. (St. Michael's Cathedral and the Russian Bishop's House were built under Etholen's leadership.) Furthermore, the missionary efforts of the Russian Orthodox Church were blossoming at this time due to the sustained financial support of the company.[26]

In spite of economic profit, however, the Russian American Company faced grave problems when it came time to renew its charter in the early 1840s. Tsar Nicholas I demurred in granting the charter in 1841, ostensibly because certain qualifications of the charter of 1821 had yet to be fulfilled. But larger political reasons may have hurt the company at this time as well. In 1825, a group of military officers proposed fundamental alterations to the autocratic Russian government that radically threatened the tsar's power. Upon the death of his brother, Tsar Aleksandr I, Nicholas ordered his troops to fire on "conspiratorial" soldiers who posed a threat to his unqualified accession to the throne. While the "Decembrist Uprising" (which occurred on December 14, 1825) was quelled, its effect on the future of the Russian American Company lingered for many years. Several conspirators, or Decembrists, were influential shareholders or members of the board of directors of the company. One was Kondratii Ryleev, a leading figure in the revolt. Nicholas ordered his troops to ransack the Russian American Company office in St. Petersburg for evidence of conspiracy. For many years, he held an uncompromising grudge against its leadership that no doubt affected the political climate that surrounded the renewal of the company's charter of operation.[27]

✦ X. THE RUSSIAN ORTHODOX CHURCH IN ALASKA ✦

Overcoming this hardship became possible because the Russian American Company continued to succeed financially. Since the 1820s, however, the tsars began to demand another requirement beyond economic profit; indeed, future renewal of the corporate charter came to depend not only on the loyalty of the company, but also on the support it gave to the mission effort of the Russian Orthodox Church. Russian state policy held the conversion of native peoples to be a vital function of the colonial presence in Alaska. Though some missionaries arrived in the New World as early as 1794, the Russian church effort lapsed after 1799 due to a lack of interest and support by the company. In that year, the first Russian Bishop in Alaska, Iosaph, died at sea enroute to Kodiak following his investiture in Irkutsk. From then until the 1820s, little official missionary activity transpired. In 1821, however, Tsar Aleksandr I mandated that the renewal of the charter granting the Russian American Company a monopoly of economic activity depended on the company's increasing its financial aid to Russian Orthodox work in Alaska. Included in this effort was to be an increase in concern for the education and welfare of native Alaskans along the lines originally stipulated by Catherine the Great.

As part of this effort, the Bishop of Irkutsk was instructed to recruit some of his best ministerial prospects to travel to the mission field of Alaska. One of the young seminarians to respond was Ivan Veniaminov. The church sent to him to Unalaska in the Aleutian Islands to serve a Russian Orthodox mission there. As with the other young priests of the White Clergy (or parish priests who were allowed to marry, as opposed to the Black Clergy who took monastic vows), Veniaminov faced unusual challenges; kayaking from village to village and learning the difficult native tongues of Alaska were two of the most intractable.

Even though his six-foot-three frame was permanently affected by being folded into the tiny kayaks, the talented Veniaminov met the challenges with great

St. Michael's Russian Orthodox Cathedral in New Archangel

success. His most noted achievement during his tenure on the Aleutian Islands (1824-1834) was his translation of the Gospel of St. Matthew and the Russian Orthodox catechism into an Aleut dialect by utilizing a variation of the Russian Cyrillic alphabet to fit Aleut linguistic patterns.[28] He also became famous in European Russia for his scientific observations, particularly on Aleutian meteorology, published in St. Petersburg under the title, *Notes on the Islands of the Unalashka District.*[29] While specially gifted as a linguist and scholar, Veniaminov was just one of a growing number of priests who were increasingly being sent to Russian America.

✦ XI. BISHOP INNOKENTII VENIAMINOV AND HIS WORK ✦

By the 1830s, the Russian Orthodox Church had expanded significantly throughout coastal Alaska. In light of this, the Holy Synod in St. Petersburg decided that a bishop was needed to govern the many parishes that had been founded. In 1839, the Synod received the tsar's approval for the institution of the office of a bishop in Alaska. Although administrative title in the Russian Orthodox Church is reserved exclusively for members of the Black Clergy, both Tsar Nicholas I and Metropolitan Philaret, the spiritual head of the church, reasoned that Veniaminov was by far the best choice to fill this role because of his knowledge and experiences in Alaska. Veniaminov went to St. Petersburg for consultation on the new proposals. Since his wife had recently died, the tsar personally requested that the renowned missionary take monastic vows and assume the leadership of the new episcopal See of Kamchatka, the Kuriles, and Aleutian Islands, a diocese which stretched from Russia's Alaskan territory across the

17

Bering Sea to mainland Asia. Veniaminov acquiesced, took the monastic name of Innokentii, and was invested as the second Russian Bishop in Alaska at the Kazan Cathedral in St. Petersburg on December 15, 1840.[30]

The Holy Synod determined that Veniaminov's episcopal seat would be at New Archangel. In preparation for his arrival, the Chief Manager of the company at the time, Arvid Etholen, began the construction of a large structure that would contain not only the living quarters of the new bishop, but also his administrative offices, a chapel, a seminary, and subsequently a parish school.[31] This structure, known as the Russian Bishop's House, welcomed Veniaminov as its first resident in 1843. Equipped with ornate wood furnishings crafted in St. Petersburg, gilded wallpaper, and valuable icons from the Orlova collection in Moscow, this massive two-story building embodied the increasing importance of the church in the life of Russia's American colony. Between 1842 and 1852, Veniaminov made three major visitations, each covering some 15,000 miles, to all the newly created parishes in his See from the home base in New Archangel. In the years after 1850, he would serve as a missionary archbishop in both Iakutsk in eastern Siberia, and

"...I visited a monastery, and afterwards the Archbishop of the place, Innokentii. The latter is one of the most distinguished, learned, and able clergymen of his Church; a celebrated preacher, with a dignified deportment, thoroughly acquainted with German theology, having formerly kept up a literary correspondence with Schleiermacher and Neander. As the salaries of the bishops are small, and he is very charitable, he would be a poor man did not the profit arising from his writings, which are popular, bring him a considerable income."

–Veniaminov, as described by Baron Von Haxthausen

Bishop Innokentii Veniaminov (in a later photo as the Metropolitan of Moscow and Kolomna)

The Russian Bishop's House in New Archangel

Blagoveshchensk-na-Amure on the Russo-Chinese border. In 1868, Tsar Aleksandr II named Veniaminov to the highest ecclesiastical position in Russia at that time, the Metropolitan of Moscow and Kolomna. From this venue, he founded the Russian Imperial Missionary Society, an organization that would raise badly-needed funds in European Russia for the missionary work in Siberia and Alaska. Upon his death in 1879, the church lauded him as one of the greatest missionaries in the history of Russian Orthodoxy.[32]

While Orthodoxy succeeded in Alaska, another denomination also held a prominent position in the Russian colony. As previously noted, Russia was a multi-ethnic nation in the eighteenth and nineteenth centuries. Thus, various nationalities were well-represented in the employ of the Russian American Company. Aside from Russians, the most notable of these were the Finns, whose expertise in ship-building and wood-working earned them valued positions in Alaska. Over time, the large Finnish contingent in New Archangel demanded their own Lutheran parish. Under the leadership of governor Etholen, also a Lutheran, the company thus brought a Finnish pastor, Uno Cygnaeus, to serve as the first Lutheran minister in the colonial capital in 1840. Not wanting competition in the mission field, Veniaminov acquiesced to this decision upon the fulfillment of various stipulations. But ecumenical relations eventually normalized, and the Lutheran community thrived in the Russian American capital.

The presence of several churches in Russian America actually served more than a religious function. As an official arm of the state, the Orthodox Church in particular played an omnibus role that impacted upon many facets of everyday life. As in Russia proper, the church provided primary education through the parish schools and had a role in the taking of the census every fifteen years. While useful to the state, church officials brought consequences that were sometimes negative as well. In many respects, the church was a vehicle for the acculturation and subjugation of the native populations to Russian rule. Overall, however, the Orthodox made a positive impact in Alaska. Indeed, the mollifying effect of clergy who were sincerely concerned about the plight of the natives generally helped to stabilize life in the colony. Particularly in Veniaminov's case, several of the church-men provided a needed tonic to the cruel actions of many of the Russians who originally came to Alaska. By respecting the culture and languages of aboriginal Alaskans, the Orthodox clerics developed a successful mission field that proved to be the most durable heritage of Russian America.[33] But prior to their appearance, a great number of the earliest arrivals set out to exploit the wilderness with little concern for native Alaskan life and culture. For many years, native Alaskans had often suffered and been indentured under arbitrary Russian control. In this regard, Russia's experience in the New World was typical of that of other European pow-ers. Over the course of the first fifty years of Russian colonization, the brutality of the newcomers was both constant and pervasive. In response, native Alaskans sometimes struck back, as the Aleuts did by massacring several Russians on Adak Island in 1764, and the Tlingit when they attacked the original Russian redoubt at Old Sitka in 1802. As time went by, relations between the Russians and the natives improved and even normalized, especially under the beneficial influence of the Russian Orthodox Church and the arrival of more educated and tolerant Russians.

✦ XII. THE SALE OF RUSSIAN AMERICA ✦

The situation nevertheless remained strained, especially at Sitka; in later years, a log stockade divided the Russian section of New Archangel from the Tlingit *ranche* that comprised the native village. In 1855, a major uprising among the Tlingit occurred over the stationing of a Russian garrison of troops sent to protect the colonial capital during the Crimean War (1853-1856). While the Russians were able to subdue this disturbance, it signified the beginning of stormier times for Russian America. The company faced not only the unhappiness of native Alaskans with elements of Russian rule, but also a serious and growing budget deficit. By the early 1850s, the Russian American Company was no longer a highly profitable venture; the numbers of sea otter had diminished due to over-hunting, and the costs of provisioning the Russian colony in Alaska began to exceed the gross income of the company. Fortunately for New Archangel and the rest of Russian America, the Crimean War itself did not take a direct physical toll on Alaskan territory. Whereas French and British ships had shelled and destroyed large sections of Petropavlovsk on the Kamchatka Peninsula, good relations between the Hudson's Bay Company and the Russian American Company helped to preserve the peace in Alaska.

Yet the Crimean War nonetheless played a significant role in the demise of Russian America on another level. Russia's shocking loss to British, French, and Turkish forces in the Black Sea exposed a nation whose reality did not support its image: Russia in the mid-nineteenth century was truly a "giant with the feet of clay." Burdened with an antiquated social structure that relied on serfdom as its basic economic support, Russia was no match for the rapidly industrializing states of Western Europe. Acceding to the throne in 1855, Tsar Aleksandr II realized that Russia's future security depended on a radical reform of its institutions. The era of

New Archangel on the eve of the sale of Alaska

the Great Reforms in Russia, including the emancipation of the serfs in 1861, arose as a corrective to Russia's backwardness (in a different yet similar way to the reformist era of Peter the Great). In the process, the Russian government turned its attention inward, and away from the borders and far fringes of an empire that was increasingly difficult to secure. The age of reform under Aleksandr II was thus accompanied by the death knell of Russian America.

The Crimean loss was of course not the only factor in the eventual removal of Alaska from the Russian Empire. Other issues played important roles as well. The emancipation of the serfs legally constrained the Russian American Company to end the unofficial exploitation of some of its native Alaskan workers. Inevitably, this hurt the company economically and pointed toward a disposal of the colony. Furthermore, British interest in the territory combined with an increasing Russian inability to defend its possessions led the tsarist government to consider a sale to a friendly third party. Even the outcome of the Opium War between Great Britain and China (1839-1842) had an effect on the decline of Russian America. With China's defeat in that war, Russia reconcentrated its efforts away from Alaska and towards the territory of the Amur and Ussuri river basins on the Manchurian border that it had ceded to a more powerful China at the Treaty of Nerchinsk in 1689.[34] The rapidly declining profitability of the Russian American Company, however, was the most pressing reason for the eventual sale of Alaska. From its inception, Russian America had been largely a commercial venture. The high costs of provisioning the territory were justifiable only by the enormous profit margins of the sea otter trade. Once that export fell off, the *raison d'etre* of the colony was lost. Just as economic potential had drawn Russians to Alaska in the 1740s, the financial decline of the Russian American Company in the 1850s marked its demise.

Beginning in the early 1850s, the Russian government sent out back-channel hints that its American territory was on the market. However, the proposed sale was fraught with diplomatic restrictions, for Russia did not want to see her colony fall into the hands of an enemy such as Great Britain, particularly in the wake of the Crimean War. Ironically, this was the country most eager to deal, for acquisition of Alaska would in effect "round out" Britain's Canadian possessions. Russia was more interested in selling to a friend, of whom the best and most obvious choice was the United States. Having enjoyed amicable relations with the U.S. for half a century, Russia pestered various elements of the American government about the sale for almost fifteen years. All the while, the tsarist foreign ministry patiently endured the U.S. Civil War and public denunciations of its territory as worthless in the halls of Congress. Privately, however, President Lincoln sent an envoy to Moscow. Finally, with the support of U.S. Secretary of State William H. Seward and likely bribes to intransigent congressmen, Russia sold Alaska to the United States in 1867 for $7.2 million.[35] In the process, a beautiful and resource-rich terrain passed from a country that wanted to get rid of it to a nation that really did not want it. For those in America who decried Alaska as "Walrussia" and "Seward's folly," only time would prove the ultimate value of Russia's former colony.

CHIEF MANAGERS OF
THE RUSSIAN AMERICAN COMPANY

1799
Emperor Paul of Russia grants the Russian American Company
an exclusive trade charter in Alaska

Aleksandr Andreevich Baranov, 1799–1818
Leontii Andreanovich Hagemeister, January–October 1818
Semen Ivanovich Ianovskii, 1818-1820
Matvei I. Muraviev, 1820-1825
Petr Egorovich Chistiakov, 1825-1830
Baron Ferdinand P. von Wrangell, 1830-1835
Ivan Antonovich Kupreanov, 1835-1840
Adolf Karlovich Etolin, 1840-1845
Mikhail D. Tebenkov, 1845-1850
Nikolai Ia. Rosenberg, 1850-1853
Aleksandr Il'ich Rudakov, 1853-1854
Stepan Vasilievich Voevodskii, 1854-1859
Ivan V. Furuhjelm, 1859-1863
Prince Dmitrii Maksoutov, 1863-1867

The list of Chief Managers of the Russian American Company is reprinted from
The Alaska Almanac, 17th edition (1993), Alaska Northwest Books, Anchorage

✢ ENDNOTES ✢

1. A number of primary documents detailing the Russian exploration of Siberia can be found in Basil Dmytryshyn, E.A.P. Crownhart-Vaughan, and Thomas Vaughan, eds., *Russia's Conquest of Siberia: A Documentary Record, 1558-1700*, Volume I (Portland, Oregon: Western Imprints, The Press of the Oregon Historical Society, 1985).

2. A.I. Alekseev, *Sud'ba russkoi ameriki* (Magadan: Magadanskoe knizhnoe izdatel'stvo, 1975), 11-17.

3. Some scholars contended that tsarist policy was the major motive force throughout the history of Russian America. See S.B. Okun', *The Russian-American Company*, trans. Carl Ginsburg (New York: Octagon books, 1979), 94.

4. N.N. Bolkhovitinov, *The Beginnings of Russian-American Relations*, trans. Elena Levin (Cambridge, Massachusetts: Harvard University Press, 1975), 146.

5. Gerhard Friedrich Muller, *Bering's Voyages: The Reports From Russia*, trans. Carol Urness (Fairbanks, Alaska: The University of Alaska Press, 1986), 69-73.

6. Ibid., 78-88 and 96-105. For further information about the First and Second Kamchatka Expeditions, see Raymond H. Fisher, *Bering's Voyages: Whither and Why* (Seattle: University of Washington Press, 1977).

7. Ibid., 148.

8. For a listing of the more famous of these original colonists, see P.A. Tikhmenev, *A History of the Russian-American Company*, trans. and ed. Richard A. Pierce and Alton S. Donnelly (Seattle: University of Washington Press, 1978), 9-11.

9. Mary E. Wheeler, "The Russian American Company and the Imperial Government: Early Phase," in S. Frederick Starr, *Russia's American Colony* (Durham, North Carolina: Duke University Press, 1987), 44-45.

10. Okun' put forth this thesis in the 1930s; over the years, other Soviet historians have supported it as well. See Okun', *The Russian-American Company*, 24-25.

11. Mary E. Wheeler, "The Origins and Formation of the Russian-American Company," Ph.D. Dissertation (1965), The University of North Carolina at Chapel Hill, 194. For a variant interpretation that views this debate from another angle, see Wheeler, "The Russian American Company and the Imperial Government: Early Phase," in S. Frederick Starr, *Russia's American Colony*, 47.

12. Hector Chevigny, *Russian America: The Great Alaskan Venture, 1741-1867* (Portland, Oregon: Binford and Mort, 1965), 59-62.

13. Tikhmenev, *A History of the Russian-American Company*, 53-55.

14. This was moreover the case since intra-Russian competition in Alaska invited unwanted foreign incursion. See R.V. Makarova, *Russians On the Pacific*, trans. and ed. Richard A. Pierce and Alton S. Donnelly (Kingston, Ontario, Canada: The Limestone Press, 1975), 162-63.

15. Shelikhov's persistence in this regard was unique among the Siberian merchants active in Alaska. See Wheeler, "The Russian American Company and the Imperial Government: Early Phase," in S. Frederick Starr, ed., *Russia's American Colony*, 47.

16. Imperial Ukaz, March 2, 1766, *Polnoe sobranie zakonov Rossiiskoi Imperii*, Vol. XVII, Number 12589, 604.

17. Hector Chevigny, *Russian America*, 122.

18. For materials on the most famous of these original monks, Herman, see Richard A. Pierce, ed., Colin Bearne, trans., *The Russian Orthodox Religious Mission in America, 1794-1837* (Kingston, Ontario, Canada: The Limestone Press, 1978).

19. Gregory Afonskii, *A History of the Orthodox Church in Alaska, 1794-1917* (Kodiak, Alaska: St. Herman's Theological Seminary Press, 1977), 64-67.

20. Basil Dmytryshyn and E.A.P. Crownhart-Vaughan, ed. and trans., *Colonial Russian America: Kyrill T. Khlebnikov's Reports, 1817-1832* (Portland: Oregon Historical Society, 1976), 106-8.

21. As with others before them, these people effectively became serfs of the company. See Svetlana G. Fedorova, *The Russian Population in Alaska and California: Late 18th Century-1867* (Kingston, Ontario, Canada: The Limestone Press, 1973), 171.

22. James R. Gibson, *Imperial Russia In Frontier America* (New York: Oxford University Press, 1976), 95.

23. Tikhmenev, *A History of the Russian-American Company*, 121-24.

24. S.G. Fedorova, V.A. Aleksandrov, eds., *Russkaia Amerika v "zapiskakh" Kirila Khlebnikova* (Moskva: Nauka, 1985), 41-44.

25. The naval officers even humiliated Baranov by auditing the financial records of the company during his tenure; Khlebnikov, who conducted the audit, completely exonerated Baranov in the end. See Chevigny, *Russian America*, 171.

26. Some historians have viewed Etholen as the most prominent Chief Manager of the Russian American Company after Baranov. See Richard A. Pierce, *Builders of Alaska: The Russian Governors, 1818-1867* (Kingston, Ontario, Canada: The Limestone Press, 1986), 22.

27. The Russian American Company destroyed part of its archives at the time of the Decembrist Uprising, presumably to protect some of the conspirators from incriminating evidence in its files. See Raymond H. Fisher, *Records of the Russian-American Company: 1802, 1817-1867* (Washington, D.C.: The National Archives, 1971), 17.

28. For vignettes of Veniaminov's life on the Aleutian Islands, see Michael Oleksa, *Orthodox Alaska: A Theology of Mission* (Crestwood, New York: St. Vladimir's Seminary Press, 1992), 127-33. See also Soterios Mousalimas, ed., *Journals of the Priest Ioann Veniaminov in Alaska, 1823-36* (Fairbanks, Alasks: University of Alaska Press, 1993).

29. Ivan Veniaminov, *Notes on the Islands of the Unalashka District*, trans. Lydia T. Black and R.H. Geoghegan (Kingston, Ontario, Canada: The Limestone Press, 1984).

30. Richard A. Pierce, "Introduction," ibid., x.

31. The major seminary of the diocese was located in New Archangel for fourteen years (1844-1858). See Basil M. Bensin, *Russian Orthodox Church In Alaska, 1794-1967* (Sitka, Alaska: Russian Orthodox Greek Catholic Church of North America, 1967), 53. Before a second building could be constructed, classes for the seminary were held on the first floor at the Russian Bishop's House.

32. Veniaminov was certainly the greatest missionary of nineteenth century Russia. See Timothy Ware, *The Orthodox Church* (London: Penguin Books, 1987), 135.

33. See Barbara Sweetland Smith, *Orthodoxy and Native Americans: The Alaskan Mission* (Crestwood, New York: St. Vladimir's Seminary Press, 1980). Refer also to Michael Oleksa, *Alaskan Missionary Spirituality* (Mahwah, New Jersey: The Paulist Press, 1987).

34. An influential group headed by Grand Duke Constantine, brother of Emperor Aleksandr II, argued strongly for the disposal of Russian America and the development of the Amur River region. See Richard A. Pierce, *Builders of Alaska*, 46.

35. Although speculative, the passing of bribes to several congressmen was probably an integral part of the ratification process needed to transfer Alaska officially from Russia to the United States. See Okun', *The Russian-American Company*, 270-71.

David J. Nordlander is the
historian at Sitka National
Historical Park in Alaska.
Over the winter, he is a Ph.D
Candidate in Russian history
at the University of North
Carolina at Chapel Hill. He is
currently working on a disser-
tation about the Gulag labor
camps of the Stalin era in
Magadan, a city across the
Bering Straits from Alaska on
the Pacific Coast of the
Russian Far East.